In Our Neighborhood

Meet a Bus Driver!

by Jodie Shepherd

Illustrations by Lisa Hunt

Children's Press®
An imprint of Scholastic Inc.

■SCHOLASTIC

Library of Congress Cataloging-in-Publication Data
Names: Shepherd, Jodie, author. | Hunt, Lisa, 1973– illustrator.
Title: In our neighborhood. Meet a bus driver!/by Jodie Shepherd; illustrations by Lisa Hunt.
Other titles: Meet a bus driver
Description: First edition. | New York: Children's Press, an imprint of Scholastic Inc., 2021. | Series: In our neighborhood | Includes index. | Audience: Ages 5–7. | Audience: Grades K–1. | Summary: "This book introduces the role of bus drivers in their community"— Provided by publisher.
Identifiers: LCCN 2021058751 (print) | LCCN 2021058752 (ebook) | ISBN 9781338768794 (library binding) | ISBN 9781338768800 (paperback) | ISBN 9781338768817 (ebook)
Subjects: LCSH: Bus drivers—Juvenile literature. | School buses—Juvenile literature.
Classification: LCC HD8039.M8 S547 2021 (print) | LCC HD8039.M8 (ebook) | DDC 388.3/22092—dc23
LC record available at https://lccn.loc.gov/2021058751
LC ebook record available at https://lccn.loc.gov/2021058752

10 9 8 7 6 5 4 3 2 1   22 23 24 25 26

Printed in Heshan, China 62
First edition, 2022

Series produced by Spooky Cheetah Press
Prototype design by Maria Bergós/Book & Look
Page design by Kathleen Petelinsek/The Design Lab

Photos ©: 7: SDI Productions/Getty Images; 11: Bob Daemmrich/Alamy Images; 12 left: Imaginechina Limited/Alamy Images; 13 left: dvdwinters/Getty Images; 13 right: David Becker/ZUMA Wire/Alamy Images; 14: Michael Matthews/Alamy Images; 16: Ben Hasty/MediaNews Group/Reading Eagle/Getty Images; 18: Alex Potemkin/Getty Images; 20: Photographerlondon/Dreamstime; 23: Bettmann/Getty Images; 25: Brian Sullivan/Barcroft Media/Getty Images.

All other photos © Shutterstock.

Table of Contents

OUR NEIGHBORHOOD

Hi! I'm Theo. This is my best friend, Emma. Welcome to our neighborhood!

gym

courthouse

pharmacy

bank

local newspaper

supermarket

dentist

veterinaria

salon

movie theater

police station

construction site

Our school is right over there. That's our bus
parked in front. Pete is our bus driver. Last Friday
was his final day on the job.

Pete has been our bus driver forever! We are really going to miss him. I made Pete a special gift to remember us by.

What do you have for Pete?

It's a memory of our time together.

About 26 million kids ride school buses in the United States. That's almost 500,000 buses!

MEET PETE

On Friday morning, Pete picked us up right on time.
As we got on the bus, we saw an adult we didn't know.

"This is Olivia," Pete told us. "She will be your new driver. Olivia is going to follow me around today. That will help her learn the job."

Most school buses in the United States are yellow so they are easy to spot. Scientists say that the human eye sees yellow faster than any other color.

We asked Pete if we could learn the job, too. He said he would teach all three of us together! Emma and I sat in the seats closest to the front.

This is going to be fun!

Pete told us that his day starts long before he gets behind the wheel.

We are all students today!

Some kids need extra help getting on and off the bus. The bus driver makes sure the wheelchair lift works smoothly and safely.

"One of our most important jobs is the walk-around," Pete explained. "We have to check the bus inside and out every day. We do that in the parking lot before and after our routes."

Bus drivers check to make sure there is enough air in the **tires.** They test the **brakes** to make sure they are working correctly.

Bus drivers make sure the **mirrors** and **windows** are clean and clear. And they check to see that the **windshield wipers** are working.

Bus drivers test the **lights** by blinking them on and off. They test the **horn** to make sure it's working, too.

Bus drivers check the **emergency exit windows** and **doors**. Those must be ready to use at any time.

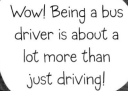

Wow! Being a bus driver is about a lot more than just driving!

A BUSY SCHOOL DAY

We were almost to the next stop. Pete started to explain everything he was doing to keep the students safe.

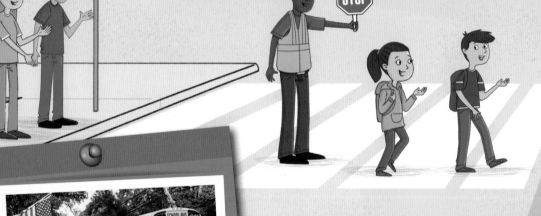

crossing arm

Some school buses have a safety crossing arm. It keeps children from walking close to the front of the bus. The driver can see them more easily.

Pete pressed a button. The bus's flashing lights went on to let other drivers know that we would be stopping. Then the stop sign arm went out on the side of the bus, and more kids got on.

Getting to school by bus pollutes the air less than getting to school by car. A bus carries more children than dozens of cars could.

Soon we arrived at school. I handed Pete my gift as I got off the bus. "Thank you, Theo," he said. "I'll see you later."

Bye, Olivia!

Our class had a field trip to the aquarium planned for that day. So Pete and Olivia came back to pick us up after math.

Some buses are big. They can fit more than 70 kids. Others are small. A group of buses is called a fleet.

It was a quick ride to the aquarium. Pete thanked me for the gift as I left the bus. He said he would be waiting for us when the field trip was over.

A few hours later, Pete dropped us back at school. "Make sure to take your things with you," he reminded everyone.

What did the ocean say to the mermaid?

Drivers make sure that all the students have gotten off the bus. They check that no kids have fallen asleep or are reading a book or playing on their phones.

Then Pete began his walk-through of the bus. He went from front to back, checking seats, closing windows, and picking up anything that had fallen on the floor. Thanks to Pete, our bus is always clean.

AFTER SCHOOL

Later that day, on the way home from school, I thought about all the other places Pete had driven us. When our baseball team won a game, Pete cheered the loudest. I was really going to miss him.

When he dropped us off, Pete said he would see us later. But he wouldn't tell us why. He said it was a surprise!

Long ago, kids who lived far from school rode horse-drawn "buses."

Later Emma's mom drove us to see Pete's surprise. We couldn't believe our eyes! Pete and a partner had opened a new food truck. It was made from an old school bus!

Old buses may be scrapped for parts. Churches or camps may use them. Some people have even turned school buses into mobile homes!

Cool!

Emma and I walked up to the window to get our food. It looked delicious. But something else caught my eye. It was the special gift I had given Pete: a picture of the three of us together!

Ask a Bus Driver

Emma asked Pete a few questions about his job.

How did you become a bus driver?

I had to show that I had a good, safe driving record. Then I had to attend a training program and get a special driver's license. I also learned basic first aid in case there's an emergency.

What's your favorite part of the job?

I really enjoy driving, and I love spending time with kids! This is the best of both worlds.

What's the hardest part of the job?

It takes practice to concentrate on the road and the traffic at the same time I'm keeping an eye on you kids.

Why do so many school buses not have seat belts?

In most states, large buses are not required to have seat belts. The buses are designed to keep kids safe by keeping riders in lots of little sections, kind of like eggs in an egg carton.

Do you drive the bus the whole day?

No, sometimes I have free time in the middle of the day. I park my bus, and then I can run an errand or visit a friend. But I'm always back before school gets out!

Pete's Tips for Riding the Bus Safely

- Leave yourself plenty of time to get to your stop so you don't have to rush.

- At pickup, stand far back from the curb until the bus comes to a complete stop and the door opens.

- Don't cross right behind or just in front of a school bus.

- Stay in your seat while riding on the bus. Keep the noise down so the driver can concentrate.

- Store your belongings out of the aisle. And don't litter. Help keep the bus clean.

- Wait until the bus is at a complete stop before getting up from your seat.

A Bus Driver's Tools

First aid kit: Bus drivers always keep a first aid kit on board in case of an accident or emergency.

Fire extinguisher: Bus drivers have a fire extinguisher mounted near the front of every school bus.

Warning triangle: Bus drivers use these devices in case the bus has to make an emergency stop on the road.

Video monitor: Some buses have video monitors to make it easier for drivers to keep an eye on their passengers.

Index

About the Author

Jodie Shepherd, who also writes under her real name, Leslie Kimmelman, is the award-winning author of dozens of fiction and nonfiction titles for children. Kimmelman loved riding the school bus when she was a student, though she had a habit of oversleeping and being the last one at her stop almost every single day.